MW00967349

A YEAR

with the

ANGELS

52 MESSAGES & 13 ESSENTIAL OIL BLENDS CHANNELED FROM THE ANGELS TO INSPIRE AND HEAL

REBECCA LOACH

CONTENTS

INTRODUCTION

If I had been told twenty years ago that I would one day write a book of channeled messages and essential oil diffuser blends, I would never have believed it. Yet life has had a funny way of guiding me to explore new adventures and discover new aspects of myself that I never imagined possible.

With a formal education in analytical sciences (a Bachelor of Science degree in Biochemistry from the University of Waterloo in Ontario, Canada), followed by a Diploma of Holistic Nutrition, I never imagined that my life would lead me into the metaphysical realms of energy healing, spiritual counselling, and channeling angels!

But here I am, twelve years after beginning my career as a Holistic Nutritionist and with over a decade of experience working in my own clinical practice, doing just that!

During my ten years in private clinical practice, I combined natural health strategies with energy healing modalities and my intuitive skills to assist clients to achieve and maintain optimal health in body, mind, and spirit.

Due to my unique perspectives on health and healing, which stemmed from my willingness to listen to what my inner knowing was telling me and to learn to trust my spiritual sight, over time I became known as a Divine Detective for health and well-being. I was able to offer support and solutions to those who were seeking relief from physical and emotional imbalances. I often helped clients who had tried many other modalities and who had worked with other health professionals to finally find relief.

My secret was to listen to the body, hold space for the voice of the innate healer within to tell us what it needs, and to put the client in a space of being able to hear and trust his or her own body's wisdom. A combination of physical nutritional counselling, natural supplements, plant medicines in the form of herbal tinctures and homeopathic preparations, energy healing, guided meditations (channeled on the spot for each client), and belief that healing can occur were my tools.

After ten years in clinical practice and a year after the birth of my son, I realized that I was no longer feeling fulfilled by my work. I wanted to reach a wider audience. I felt the pull to serve in a bigger way than what I had been doing.

I began to build a business online, focused on sharing the spiritual and channeled messages that I had found to be so effective for my clients' healing, and to guide people to tap into their own spiritual wisdom. I led online healing circles, offered private intuitive readings for clients - which included recommendations for supporting the physical body and energetic/spiritual healing - and created and launched my first deck of healing cards: the Angelic Alchemy Essence Card deck.

In January 2017, after returning from a powerful trip to the island of Maui, I received Divine guidance to channel weekly messages from the angels and send them out via email to those on my mailing list. I started as soon as I returned home and have not missed a single "Monday morning message" since. No matter where I am, how I am feeling, or what I am doing, I always show up for these Divine assignments and allow the messages to flow through me and out into the world for those who are meant to hear them.

A few months after returning home from Maui, I reconnected with a beautiful soul who was also attending the same retreat that I was. We chatted about essential oils and she offered to send me some samples. I had been exposed to doTERRA essential oils before and wasn't interested, but there was something about the timing and the fact that this beautiful soul had a similar background to me – a combination of science, natural health, and spiritual insight – that had me agreeing to give them a try. Little did I know, my life was about to change again.

As soon I opened the envelope I had collected from my mailbox a week later, I dumped the contents – six small vials of essential oils – into my hand and could immediately feel the energy of these oils. My hand began to vibrate and I knew I held something special. I had never felt this same vibration from any of the other essential oils that I had tried.

Over the next few months, I watched my health improve from the use of these oils, and, even more unexpectedly, the energy and vibe of our home and our family unit shifted. More peace. More connection. More joy in every aspect of our family life. My intuition and connection to the angelic realms took another quantum leap. I knew I had to share these oils with others.

I began to teach essential oil classes in addition to my work as an energetic and intuitive healer. I continued to write my weekly Messages from the Angels, but now had the beautiful scents of doTERRA essential oils misting from my diffuser as I channeled. My experience of the angels and of my higher self became richer and deeper. More peace and awareness began to flow into my days.

Then, one day, I was told it was time to turn these channeled messages into a book – a book you now hold in your hands.

Fifty-two messages, one for each week of the year, are contained in this book. The messages have been expanded upon in certain places, as the angels provided a bit more information during the editing process. In a few spots, grammar has been cleaned up slightly to improve readability, however, I have tried to keep the messages as intact as possible, exactly as they came through my fingers during the channeling process.

It was always my intention to include a few essential oil blends in the back of this book to help promote healing and inspiration from the plant kingdom, however, just as I was about to send the final manuscript to my editor, I began to receive more "downloads" of information, this time healing blends to match the essence of these channeled writings.

Three days of writing oil blends sent to me by the angels, plus the energetic information on how to use them and what properties they provide, testing them to make sure they smelled okay (some of them sounded quite strange to me when I wrote them out and my human mind wanted to be sure none of them were truly offensive to the nose), and finally the manuscript was complete.

It is my intention that you find peace, connection, and empowerment within the words on these pages, and that you immerse yourself in the energy of the angels, our beautiful gifts of the earth represented in the essential oil blends, and that you remember your greatness.

Blessings,

Rebecca Loach

July 2018

HOW TO USE THIS BOOK – WHAT TO EXPECT

This book is comprised of fifty-two channeled messages, representing a complete year of my weekly channeled Messages from the Angels.

You may wish to create sacred space for yourself on the same day each week when you grab a cup of tea, curl up in your favourite chair, turn on your essential oil diffuser, play gentle music, and open your heart and mind as you read these sacred messages.

Or, you may want to read this book all in one sitting, or flip though it when it feels right, or use it as an "oracle," asking for Divine guidance and opening to a page at random to receive your message.

There is no one way to use this book. Do what feels best for you.

You can return to these messages again and again. They never lose their importance and effectiveness at bringing you into alignment with your higher energy and reminding you of the greatness of who you are.

As you read each message, notice what you feel, sense, imagine, or think about. Each message contains energetic transmissions and healing activations within the words. You may notice a gentle tingling in your body or new insights and awareness as you read the words. Or you may feel nothing at all. Know that whatever you experience is just right, and the angels are working with you in subtle ways whether you are aware of it or not.

In certain places, you will find key phrases **bolded and italicized**. These phrases are often posed as questions that would be great journal prompts for further exploration and self-discovery.

Periodically, you'll find a new diffuser blend that captures the energy and essence of the message before it. There are also instructions on how to make your own roller ball blend, should you choose to wear your oils topically instead of diffusing them.

If you are used to using essential oil blends topically, you may find that the recipes for the roller ball blends are more dilute than the ones you're used to. This is by design as it allows the oils and energy of the plant medicines to act on your energetic body, allowing space for the body to rise up and meet the energy of your soul. A gentler approach creates space for this connection to occur. Trust the process. You will be amazed at the transformations that will occur!

You may choose to work with a particular essential oil blend for a set amount of time or interchange them as your energy and inspiration suits you. There is no right or wrong way to read this book or to use these blends.

Be aware of your emotions, thoughts, insights, and synchronicities that happen in your life after using these essential oil blends. Using these blends in combination with the accompanying intentions is powerful for spiritual transformation and evolution!

Should you desire to know more about essential oils and the oils that I was guided to use by the angels, you will find a link to join my essential oil community and to work with me personally at the back of this book.

A Note on Essential Oil Safety

These blends have only been tested with doTERRA essential oils, which are the oils I was guided to work with by the angels after trying several other brands. I cannot guarantee the same results with any other brand of essential oils.

Please refer to manufacturer's safety information for safe use of essential oils. If you are pregnant, nursing, or have a specific health condition or concern, please consult a qualified healthcare practitioner.

1

A COSMIC WASHING

Let us begin with a Cosmic Washing – a clearing of all that you are now ready to shift and transform. For, you see, it is time for you to forgive the past and move forward into the present to create the future that is filled with all the potentials you hold within.

And so we begin...

Let it go...let go of all the fear, the pain, and the discontent that you hold within your body, within your cells, and within your very being.

Allow, in this moment, all of the pain and suffering you have ever experienced to be washed away, as if by a cosmic washing, a rolling wave that comes through your being now.

Allow this sacred water to wash over you; feel the cool water entering into every crevice, every corner, every hollow, every cell, organ, and tissue.

Feel this water wash over your body, your mind, your emotions, and your entire being, cleansing away with it any feelings of sorrow, pain, worry, grief, trauma, or memories that you are ready to release.

Washing, shining, polishing...

Feel the renewal, the enlightened energy that is now available. Allow it to come forward, no longer hidden or pushed aside by this darkness.

Know that you *are* this light...this is you. Hold this light in your awareness, and allow yourself to *be*.

Contemplate what it means to be this being of newly washed light and energy.

Who will you now be, without this debris holding you back?

You are safe, and you are loved. Always.

~ The Angelic Realm

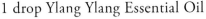

SACRED WATERS DIFFUSER / ROLLER BALL BLEND

1 drop Ylang Ylang Essential Oil
2 drops Melissa Essential Oil
1 drop Clary Sage Essential Oil

This diffuser blend sets the tone for a higher vibration in your energy field. It calls upon the energy of sacred water and envelops you in healing light and love as you wash away the pain, fear, and lower emotions that are holding you back from becoming the best version of yourself.

To make a 5mL roller ball blend to wear topically, add the drops of oil to a 5mL roller bottle, then top with fractionated coconut oil (or other carrier oil). Apply over your heart, abdomen, and back of the neck in the morning or evening.

When diffusing or using this blend topically, take a moment to feel, sense, imagine, or think about the sacred water flowing over you, connecting with your energy field and washing away all the debris you are ready to release.

Repeat this daily for fourteen days, either diffusing or by applying the roller ball blend topically and notice how your life transforms.

A look at the oils in this blend:

Ylang Ylang – The Oil of the Inner Child. This oil acts mainly on the heart energy, releasing negative feelings and heavy-heartedness. It restores you to a feeling of childlike innocence and openness.

Melissa – The Oil of Light. This oil helps to release all forms of blocks that may be holding you back and awakens your soul to its truth and light.

Clary Sage – The Oil of Clarity and Vision. This oil assists in clearing blocks and dispelling darkness, while encouraging and clarifying spiritual vision.

2
SURRENDER

We look upon you without judgment. Nothing you could ever feel, think, do, or say could change the love and compassion that we hold for you.

You are part of us, part of the great majestic energy of the One.

When you let go and surrender, you are not letting go of control, as you fear you will be…you are surrendering into an allowance of a new form of conscious living.

When you surrender and let go of trying to make things happen just the way you think they ought to, you open up to the potential for things to turn out in ways that are bigger and better than you ever imagined possible.

The art of letting go, of surrender (spiritually-speaking), is not about giving up control and letting someone else or something else guide your life. Spiritual surrender is letting go of the egoic mind…of not letting this false ego control you anymore.

You see, the very control you think you have is the thing that is controlling you.

As you step away from the control of your ego, the mind that tells you what to think and how to be (all based out of fear, you see), you are able to access the higher guidance system of your being.

It is here that we, in the angelic realms, can merge with you more easily.

When you surrender the struggle between you and your ego-mind, you open yourself up to more of the fullness of your Divine self.

This self knows all; it knows the way. It knows your joys, your dreams, your purpose, and your best path forward. This is where we sit in communion with you and we are able to communicate more easily without the barriers of the ego-mind interfering.

We can rejoice together, sharing the energy of love and of pure potential as we create a life together that serves the greatest good of all.

This is something that the ego-mind can never fathom.

So you see, dear one, surrender is not about giving up control and allowing yourself to be guided by someone or something else, it is about opening up to the fullness of who you are, and allowing *you* to be guided by more of *you*!

We rejoice in the energy and presence of *you* in this place of love and peace and pure exalted joy. **Will you join us?**

~ The Angelic Realm

3

YOUR PIECE OF THE PUZZLE

You are here, in this moment, right now, playing an important role.

You see the world around you and you may ask, "What is happening?" and "What can I do?"

We tell you that you are doing it, right now, as you are being you!

When you listen and follow the inner guidance, the inner voice of your heart calling you forth, you are doing your part.

All the pieces of the puzzle are falling into place, and everyone must play their part.

Some of the puzzles fit together nicely, and some of the pieces seem to belong to another puzzle, an older puzzle – one that doesn't seem to work anymore.

Yet those pieces are still here…they, too, are playing their parts.

What are you to do?

Continue being the beautiful, bright, brilliant piece of the puzzle that you have always been.

Listen more deeply into your own knowing and find the beauty of the unique shapes, curves, and connections that you bring to the bigger puzzle, the puzzle of inter-connectedness and humanity in conscious evolution.

Know that when you go about your day, doing the things that you do as you, you are contributing to the entire energy of the puzzle.

Every piece is needed. Every piece is valued.

You do not serve the greater good by trying to force yourself to fit where you do not.

You are perfect, whole, and complete just as you are – when you rest, when you enjoy simple pleasures, when you spend time with friends and family, when you spend time in self-reflection, when you work, when you write, when you speak out. All these actions and moments of stillness, which come from your heart, contribute to the bigger puzzle that is being formed and shaped as it has always done.

Do not doubt your importance.

As you listen and follow the guidance of your heart, you are contributing to the whole. Whether this means action or stillness, your piece matters.

When you can stop trying to force yourself into another shape that you feel is more important, more needed, or more valuable than you think you are, you allow yourself to find your unique and perfect fit.

We say again – you are perfect just as you are. Made for this place. Made for this time. Made as you.

We honour you and your place in this rich, multidimensional, ever-evolving puzzle of human consciousness.

~ The Angelic Realm

4

YOUR CREATIVE LIFE

Creativity is not a measure of how many paintings, songs, speeches, or pieces of art you have created, but rather your ability to open up and listen to the voice and messages of power that exist within you.

You each hold a measure of creative potential. This is the ability to create beautiful works in the world.

Whether this is through art, through acts of kindness, or through your ability to speak and read and walk…all of this is creative energy set in motion.

Every thought, every emotion, and every action comes from this creative energy. It's how you learn to channel it through your being that matters.

As you open and awaken the creative centre within you, located below your navel, you can access more and more of this potential; your actions, your emotions, and your words then have a greater impact in the world.

You become adept at moving more gracefully, you become a greater wordsmith, you are able to see the world through different eyes...the possibilities open to you and you can see how to *create* new worlds.

Create with inspired action. Create through loving thought. Create through a gentle touch, a helping hand, or a supportive glance.

All of this is creativity. It is allowing the energy and majesty of you as a creator and as one who was created to flow through and into the world.

The more you can let go of seeing creativity as some skill to be had or honed, the more you can open up to the massive creative potential that exists within you and is just waiting to come out.

Focus on the energy in your belly. Feel the energy as a glowing ball of golden light. Allow yourself to listen to the sound that this area makes as it aches to be free. Allow yourself to see the light and its brightness. Allow this energy to build up...to grow...and to overflow out into the world.

As you sit in this energy, you open and connect with the higher energies of creation and you become more of your Divine self.

And then, you, dearest soul, can bring that creative spark back to the planet and manifest it in your life in bigger ways.

Be open to the possibilities and be willing to redefine your definition of what it means to be creative.

You, by your very nature and existence, were born creative.

How will you wield your creativity? We can't wait to find out.

~ The Angelic Realm

AWAKENED CREATIVITY DIFFUSER / ROLLER BALL BLEND

1 drop Wild Orange Essential Oil
2 drops Tangerine Essential Oil
1 drop Spearmint Essential Oil

This diffuser blend awakens creativity and inspires confidence in how you communicate your unique gifts in the world. Use this oil blend whenever you are feeling stifled creatively or weighed down by the humdrum of day-to-day life. It will instantly uplift your energy and open a portal to your higher knowing so you can return to feeling alive and inspired.

To make a 5mL roller ball blend to wear topically, add the drops of oil to a 5mL roller bottle, then top with fractionated coconut oil (or other carrier oil). Apply to your temples, wrists, and lower abdomen.

When diffusing or using this blend topically, take a moment to tune into your second chakra, the energy centre located about two inches beneath the navel. Feel, sense, imagine, or think about energy building up in this area and spilling out into the world. Then notice what thoughts, ideas, and inspirations you receive and act on them. The more you practice tuning into your creative potential, the more easily it will flow in your day-to-day life, bringing you a greater sense of joy, meaning, and purpose.

A look at the oils in this blend:

Wild Orange – The Oil of Abundance. This oil inspires creativity and uplifts your mood. It helps to release the mindset of lack and scarcity and restores feelings of joy and flow in your life.

Tangerine – The Oil of Cheer and Creativity. This oil instantly uplifts your mood and opens the doors for creative flow.

Spearmint – The Oil of Confident Speech. This oil helps you express your "voice" in the world. It aids you in expressing your creative energy with confidence and clarity.

5

ALIGNING WITH YOUR SOUL'S PLAN

Y ou have everything you need to accomplish all that
you have set out for yourself.

Plan. Prepare. Take action. *Then surrender.*

Allow us to hold you and carry your creations to the world.
Trust that you are being guided.

Whenever you feel tense, anxious, or tight in your body, it's
a sure sign that you are holding on and seeking to control
the outcome.

In these moments, let go!

Let go of the struggle against yourself; instead surrender
into the flow of the Divine that you carry within.

Allow yourself to merge with your higher presence and
higher purpose, for it knows the way.

When you come up against these walls, ask yourself, *"How can I surrender?"* Then allow yourself to clear your mind and body of thoughts and fear.

Allow yourself to float on the energy of being cared for and nurtured. Allow yourself to rest in the arms of the angels. Feel us near, guiding you along your path – the path that you have laid out for yourself before you came into being on the planet.

We will guide and support you to realize the truth that you came here to experience.

In this space, you will open to receive new insights, ideas, and inspirations. This is the true essence of creative flow and process. It is where you will be open to all your abilities and faculties, and the ability to channel more of your Divine nature into everything you do.

This is where *things get done.*

If you are feeling lost, confused, or not productive, we say again *surrender* and allow yourself to open up to the fullness of what is possible.

Your limited mind is trying to create a path based on your experience and understanding of the world.

Your infinite self knows all the possibilities.

Allow yourself to let go of control and the limitations of your ego-mind and open up to the possibilities that are available when you connect more deeply to the truth of who you are.

All you have to do is rest and open up to the energy of comfort and support that is all around you. Imagine yourself in a warm embrace.

Then wait.

The light will come and you will see the path forward.

~ The Angelic Realm

6

YOU ARE INFINITELY SUPPORTED

Every thought, action, emotion, and desire is held in our care.

If only you would allow yourself to see the help that is available to you to achieve your dreams, your goals, and your immediate needs...your life would begin to flow in immeasurable ways.

When you feel lost, afraid, alone, or unsupported we ask you to stop, breathe, and awaken your senses.

Allow your mind and all your senses to expand and feel the energy and the threads of the Universe all around you. Notice the peaceful, calming, nurturing, and supportive elements of this energy, waiting just beyond your physical self. Immerse yourself in it.

Imagine yourself reaching out to touch these threads, to swirl them in your fingers. Imagine what you can create with these threads. Allow the energy of support to flow into your being.

Ask for what you need.

Give voice to your fears and allow yourself to fully comprehend the depths of your need.

Then release that need to us. Trust that you are heard. And open yourself up to the energy of support that is available.

It is in the acknowledgment of your pain that you are able to let it go. And then it is in the faith that you are supported that you are able to open up and allow us to help you.

Get out of your own way.

Do not loop your thoughts on your fears, wishing you could find a way out. Acknowledge them and share them with us, then decide that you will shift them.

Watch for the signs, opportunities, and choices that present themselves to you.

There is always a way. Let us guide you.

We rejoice when you ask for help because we love you and we can't intervene until you ask us to. So, get out of your own way and be willing to receive all the blessings that you desire and that you deserve.

You are infinitely supported. Will you believe it?

~ The Angelic Realm

7

CREATING FREEDOM

Today, do whatever you can to bring more freedom into your life. Declutter, play, sing, dance, scratch something off your to-do list. Break all the restrictions you have placed upon yourself.

Ask yourself: *What feels good? Then do it.*

Too much of your energy is spent believing there are certain tasks you must do in order to be deemed worthy or productive. These beliefs drain your energy and pull you out of alignment from your truth – that you are worthy by your very presence on earth, that you are deserving of all that you desire, that you are productive when you tune into the energy of your heart and follow its guidance unceasingly.

The wisdom of your heart calls you to shine today and allow the energy of love, joy, abundance, light, and freedom to flow from you.

Close your eyes and listen. Can you hear the pulse? Can you feel the beat?

Listen, and you will find us there, ready to rejoice in the freedom of creation, which has been waiting for you.

~ The Angelic Realm

8

HIGHER EVOLUTIONARY STAGE

As you enter this new golden era that is set out before you, each moment counts more and more. *Will you choose the energy of freedom, of expansion, and of soul growth? Or will you continue to do things as you have always done?*

We tell you that it is time to embrace this evolutionary change.

You are safe. You are whole. You are complete.

As you learn to let go of the conditioning that humanity has been under for the last many centuries, and instead choose to listen to the higher voice of Source and self, you will find that miracles begin to happen. Synchronicities, new opportunities, and new awarenesses will present themselves repeatedly to you when you place yourself in an open position to observe and allow them into your life.

We are surrounding you with love and light, as we always have. You are now at a higher evolutionary stage and you are able to hear us more than ever before.

It is in the stillness, in times of joy, pure love, happiness, and fun that you are able to open the gateway to the higher self and connect with us more deeply.

We say to you – *be*! Have fun. Do what brings you joy. Be free. Everything will fall into place.

The coulds, shoulds, and have-tos of the past no longer hold you. Allow yourself to break free and see what is possible when you awaken to the world of love, joy, and openness. You will find us there, along with all the dreams you have held along the way.

The journey is unfolding. How fun and exciting and joyful are you willing to make it?

~ The Angelic Realm

HIGHER EVOLUTION DIFFUSER / ROLLER BALL BLEND

1 drop Tangerine Essential Oil
1 drop Wild Orange Essential Oil
2 drops Bergamot Essential Oil
1 drop Peppermint Essential Oil

This diffuser blend raises you up to higher octaves of energetic presence. The combination of three citrus oils (a trinity) plus a mint creates a very high energetic vibration. This blend calls in the energy of synchronicity and abundant living. It puts you in an energetic vibration where it is easier to believe in and attract miracles. With attention and intention, your life can change rapidly when you use this blend.

To make a 5mL roller ball blend to wear topically, add the drops of oil to a 5mL roller bottle, then top with fractionated coconut oil (or other carrier oil). Apply to the crown of your head, temples, back of your neck, and base of your spine. This will create a beautiful alignment of your Divine energy patterns, connecting your brain and nervous system energies to that of your core energy.

When diffusing or using this blend topically, take a moment to focus on the energy of your head, imagining an octahedron shape from your crown, to your temples at the side of your head, to the base of your skull, then flowing in a line down your back to the base of your spine.

Feel, sense, imagine, or think about energy of golden light and potential flowing in these areas, activating the highest expression of you. Feel your power and invite your Divine self to be present as you go about your day.

A look at the oils in this blend:

Wild Orange – The Oil of Abundance. This oil inspires creativity and uplifts your mood. It helps to release the mindset of lack and scarcity and restores feelings of joy and flow in your life.

Tangerine – The Oil of Cheer and Creativity. This oil instantly uplifts your mood and opens the doors for creative flow.

Bergamot – The Oil of Self-Acceptance. This oil releases stagnant energy and limiting beliefs and promotes feelings of self-love and self-acceptance. It is a beautiful oil to help remind you of the powerful, unlimited being you are.

Peppermint – The Oil of a Buoyant Heart. This oil uplifts the body, mind, and spirit and helps you to rise above emotional pain. It provides strength and clarity to overcome your limitations and challenges.

9

A HEART PAUSE

If something that once brought you joy, love, and filled you up no longer does, do not immediately assume you are on the wrong path.

If your heart is not in what you are doing anymore, it may not mean that it is time to give up and search for something new. It may simply mean that your heart needs a pause, a rest, and time to catch up with the magnificent changes that are happening in your world right now.

Believing that you need to let go and run to the next thing that lights up your heart is a trick of the ego-mind. It will take every advantage it can to keep you feeling in control. It will tell you that following your heart means dropping everything and rushing to the next thing that brings you joy. It keeps you in the game of pushing, searching, striving, and grasping for more.

Instead of allowing more love, more joy, more peace, and more abundance to come to you as you naturally follow the guidance of your soul, your ego-mind will trick you into believing that you need to go out and seek these things out, or you will never have them.

Life is a balance – letting go of what no longer serves but not rushing to throw away things that may be in a period of pause and in a resting and recalibration phase at the moment.

Before you give up and search for something new, allow yourself to pause and ask: *What brings me ultimate joy? What will fill my heart now? What can bring me that sense of peace in this moment, this present moment, here and now?*

Then allow yourself to experience that. Immediately. And let the rest sit for a moment. Let it be where it is. Do not make any hasty decisions.

As you allow yourself the time and the space to see where things are and to catch your breath on an energetic level, your heart will once again begin to speak and to guide you in the direction you are to go. It just needs a moment to catch up and find itself again in this new evolutionary phase you are entering now.

Surrender. Trust. Have Faith.

~ The Angelic Realm

10

BECOME A MASTER OF LOVE

You were chosen for this life. You were chosen to come to this earth and have these experiences so that you could know and understand what it means to live as a human.

The human life is an intricate dance, a dance of dualities – light and dark, love and hate, hope and despair.

Learning to manage and rise above this duality, to see from a higher perspective, and to touch into the energy of pure love, that is the task set before you.

As you go throughout your daily life, your job is to look at what is going on around you and to see the illusions – **what have you told yourself in your mind is true?**

As you take another look, opening your heart and your mind to the energy of Divine and perfect love – **what do you see is now true? What is possible that was not possible before?**

Know that it is all a matter of perspective. ***Do you choose to live in the energy of chaos or to live in the energy of freedom?***

"Easier said than done," you may say, and we know this. We ask of you, in this now time, to put this exercise into practice. ***Look around and ask yourself, "What is real?"***

Here you will find freedom. You will be able to rise above the duality - rise above the good versus bad, right versus wrong, light versus dark - and see that the energy of love permeates all things. Then you can choose to follow this thread of love and weave more of it into your daily life.

It really is that simple.

How do you become a master of love? Practice. Practice every day. Soon you will be a natural!

~ The Angelic Realm

11
JUST LIKE YOU

All the masters who have come before you shared the same struggles as you do now – to know themselves and to know God (Creator, Source, Spiritual Energy, the One).

Those you read about doing great works were just like you. The only difference is that they remembered their truth and found their sense of purpose and focused on it with clear attention and intentions. They rose above fear and found the courage and strength to do what they came here to do.

You can, too.

Reach out and ask us for help to remember. Allow us to fill you with the loving support, confidence, and faith that you may feel you are lacking at times. When you are afraid or feel lost, lean on us for support.

Once you ask and express your desire to awaken, we can begin to work with you at a higher level. We will send you codes of enlightenment – sacred wisdom and knowledge of who you are and why you came to Earth. Together, we can unfold the fabric of your life and lift you up to the realms of the Earth angels.

We do this with joy, for that is our task – to help you remember yours and to guide you and hold you through the journey to remembering your greatness.

~ The Angelic Realm

12

THE FORGOTTEN WAY

Have you forgotten your way? Have you lost faith? Do you not know how great you are?

Breathe.

Open your heart and allow us to show you.

Trust.

You are safe.

The golden light of your power and truth flows from your heart and solar plexus energies out into the Universe.

This line of bright light is like a golden thread in the infinite tapestry of the Universe. It is your connection to the Divine source of all.

Dancing in this golden light are sacred symbols that spell out your name and your story. Like words of a sentence that grow to a paragraph and then a novel, so, too, do these symbols tell the story of you.

These "words" and this light are always here, even when you forget or refuse to see them. It doesn't change a thing, for you were made in this light.

When you forget or feel lost, breathe. Focus. Remember.

Realign with this golden light and you will once again find your way.

Call on us for help. We are always here to guide and support you on your way. We've got you.

~ The Angelic Realm

Sacred Devotion Diffuser / Roller Ball Blend

1 drop Cedarwood Essential Oil
1 drop Frankincense Essential Oil
2 drops Sandalwood Essential Oil

This diffuser blend envelops you in the grounded, earthy, and uplifting energy of sacred devotion. It helps you to cut through the fears and illusions of the mind and return to a state of humility, faith, and gratitude. It restores you to the presence of the Divine and the flow of the Divine in you.

To make a 5mL roller ball blend to wear topically, add the drops of oil to a 5mL roller bottle, then top with fractionated coconut oil (or other carrier oil). Apply to your heart, wrists, and the soles of your feet.

When diffusing or using this blend topically, take a moment to give gratitude for your presence here on Earth, and for the presence of the Divine walking beside you. Feel, sense, imagine, or think about the connection you have with the energy of the earth and the energy of the cosmos. Know that you are protected and watched over always.

This is a great blend to use when you are feeling lost, alone, or afraid, as it will help guide you home. This also is a great blend to use for daily spiritual practice, or when you want to take your prayer, meditation, or journaling to a deeper level.

A look at the oils in this blend:

Cedarwood – The Oil of Community. This oil reminds you that you are part of a greater community and that you are never alone. It inspires feelings of faith, belonging, and connection.

Frankincense – The Oil of Truth. This oil helps to dissolve the lies and illusions that keep you trapped and hold you back from living life to the fullest. It connects you back to your Divine light.

Sandalwood – The Oil of Sacred Devotion. This oil helps to quiet the mind and assists you in hearing the voice of the Divine. It aids in releasing ties and attachment to the material world and to feel connected to the energy of All That Is.

13

SPACE FOR YOUR DREAMS

We are giving you all of the tools, clarity, and focus that you need to walk forward and make the next level of your desires come true.

The more you clear and declutter your environment and mind, the more easily you can hear, see, and feel us. When you remove the earthly distractions that call to your mind to notice, you can more deeply tune into the energy of All That Is.

You do not need to give away all your earthly possessions, we merely suggest that you remove any objects, items, or activities that serve to keep your mind busy with overwhelm, anxiety, and mind-chatter. Keep only those things that give you a feeling of being uplifted and carry the resonance of joy, peace, and love.

Everything around you is energy and affects your vibration.

When you feel in a state of unrest, confusion, or anxiety, take a breath and look around with fresh eyes. **What is contributing to this feeling? What distractions are around** *you that are pulling your mind toward negativity, sadness, or fear?*

First comes thought, then comes emotion, then comes action.

Everything you see with your physical eyes creates a thought in your mind, whether you realize it or not. How you think about these things affects how you feel. How you feel will affect your ability to manifest and create in the world. For it is a spiral – like attracts like. Positive thoughts create positive feelings, which attract positive things into your life.

Remove the distractions. Create space for breath in your life. Feel the energy of freedom flow through your being as you release that which is weighing you down. You will be astounded at what a difference it makes.

Make space for Spirit to enter your life. Clearing your environment clears your mind. This in turn affects your emotions and allows us to enter into communion more freely with you.

All that you seek is within your grasp. See freedom. Surround yourself with joy. We will be with you always.

~ The Angelic Realm

14
ALREADY YOURS

You are entering a new phase of your life. We could say this to you every day, because it is true.

As you go through your day today, feel the truth of this statement. Act as though the new, exciting phase is beginning. Because it is.

As you look around your life today with fresh eyes, notice all the signs and opportunities that surround you to create exactly what you want in your life. All the threads are there – the beginning steps to achieving your dreams and goals.

And you know what, dear one? They have always been there. You just haven't noticed. We have placed everything that you desired within your reach, ready for you to claim for yourself. It's just a matter of noticing.

Today, we ask you to look. See. Notice the beginning of the path that will take you to the full manifestation of your dreams. Be aware. Express gratitude. Then accept these blessings.

We want you to have everything you desire. You just have to accept that you are worthy and it is possible.

We love you. ***Can you love yourself enough to claim what is already yours?***

~ The Angelic Realm

15

THE POWER OF YOUR AUTHENTIC SELF

Your authenticity is your greatest asset. No one can express your unique energetic frequency but you.

You carry within you the wisdom of All That Is, locked away and secreted into your care. Every single human walking the earth right now carries the same secrets; however, not many are able to rise above the illusion and duality of the human mind and tap into this truth, which you carry within your very being.

When you connect with your inner truth, you are able to rise above the crowd and follow the compass of your soul and the code of your heart. You translate the secrets that you carry into your own vibrational expression of them, and this allows you to play an important role in the development of the collective consciousness of your planet.

For, you see, you were meant to come here and express this ultimate truth, which you carry inside of you in your unique way so you can help break through the noise of the collective unrest.

Your unique way of speaking – of voicing your opinions, of carrying your energy, of sharing your message – is exactly what the world needs. A multitude of different ways of speaking this ultimate truth will allow more people to hear.

To show up and to live life by your values, your moral code, and expressing your unique qualities...*this is real power*. This is the expression of your unique version of the secrets you carry.

Never doubt that showing up just as you are is good enough. In fact, it's the most powerful expression of love and energy that exists.

You are infinitely protected and loved. We walk beside you, supporting and cheering you on along the way.

~ The Angelic Realm

16

THE GLORIOUS NATURE
OF WHO YOU ARE

All of these tools, rituals, and practices that you set up for yourself are merely mind-driven ways to get you to connect more closely to God and to Source energy. This does not make them bad or ineffective, as the mind is a powerful part of your creation and incarnation, which is required for your continual development and forward movement on the human-earth plane.

The true value in these tools, rituals, and practices is the emotional or heart-connection that is created. In other words, it is about how you feel, what you believe, and the *faith* that you pour into them.

When you come from a place of having a deep desire to connect and to know God (Source – Divine) these tools, rituals, and practices act like a medium through which your mind and your physical body can create an opening. It is here that you can open up to the infinite flow and connection with All That Is.

Spiritual practices and traditions are powerful. And they are made more powerful by the numbers of people who practice them together. In unity, in collective consciousness, a powerful energy field is created that creates a mark or an imprint.

When you are practicing these rituals and traditions, you are entering into the flow of this energy imprint, and thus are being carried along the path. It's a powerful process.

And we say to you…it doesn't matter *how* you practice, as long as your heart is pure, your desire is there, and your ultimate goal is to seek and to know more of who you are and your beautiful place in the Divine plan.

We also say to you: it is okay to not follow precisely. If you are feeling guided to practice differently, to connect differently, or to find new ways that fit with you, that is equally powerful.

And we would say to you that this may be even more powerful as you are entering into a new age, where your individual contributions will help empower the whole.

No longer are you meant to walk in a singular path, but to paint the world with the colours, the frequencies, the vibrations, and the glorious nature of who you are.

It is only in honouring the individual as part of the whole that the collective can come back into unity and what it once was again.

We honour you, and all of your offerings on your path to remembering.

~ The Angelic Realm

CREATING DIVINE CONNECTION

Which tools, rituals, and practice help you feel empowered and connected to your true self and the Divine?

Which tools, rituals, and practices do you use out of fear, obligation, or guilt (past or present)?

What are you now ready to let go of, in favour of following what feels good and aligned for you?

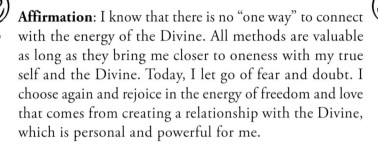

Affirmation: I know that there is no "one way" to connect with the energy of the Divine. All methods are valuable as long as they bring me closer to oneness with my true self and the Divine. Today, I let go of fear and doubt. I choose again and rejoice in the energy of freedom and love that comes from creating a relationship with the Divine, which is personal and powerful for me.

17

YOU ARE LOVED, ALWAYS

We say to you today how very proud we are of you. Through all that you have experienced, all that you have accomplished, all that you are, and all that you will be.

Nothing could ever change that. Nothing.

No matter how far you may have strayed from the path, you are loved. No matter how virtuous you have been, you are loved.

We love you equally for your faults and your virtues.

You are part of the whole, part of the One, part of us, and we are a part of you. Divine love is unconditional.

So, when you look upon your life and see things that you feel are a stain on your existence, remember we see them only as a blip, a nanosecond (actually less) in the time-continuum of existence.

They are not forever. They are less than an instant, then gone, and a new moment is available to create a new path.

No matter what you have done, you are loved. No matter what you will do, you are loved.

Now can you turn that same love upon yourself?

We think you can. ***Give it a try.***

~ The Angelic Realm

18

OVERCOMING FEAR ENERGY

All that you have been experiencing these past few months has been the overcoming and the releasing of fear energy.

As you step into a new way of being, the old must first be cleared. This means that in times of peace and rest, as you are evolving forward, old clutter and debris will have space to rise up, for you are ready and able to release and transform it once and for all.

You may be tempted to hold onto this clutter. These old beliefs, thoughts, and patterns in your life have become comfortable; they are part of you. And we say to you, do not be afraid any longer. It is safe to let them go. It is time. You will not be able to progress any farther upon your spiritual path if you still have this old clutter weighing you down.

Take a deep breath. Breathe this truth into your heart. Feel the breath from the top of your head through your entire body. Feel the strength and the presence of the Divine within you and all around you as you prepare for the next step of your evolution.

Then affirm: "I am ready to move forward. I am ready to let go of the old to make way for the new."

Fear will come up at times – uncertainty, lack of faith, and a wavering of trust. Release judgment of this...it's part of the process. As you unravel the layers of the past that you have held within your cells, you will be shedding this fear and leaving it behind.

Affirm: "I am supported and guided by the Divine in all ways. I am ready to step into the glory of who I am."

Notice the fear, the judgment, and the uncertainty. Then simply let it go, making space for the next level of debris to be released.

In this, you will find freedom. And so it is.

~ The Angelic Realm

19

BOTH HUMAN AND DIVINE

Dear human: Why are you so hard on yourself?

We address you as human first to remind you that it is the "human" part of you that sits in judgment; the "human" part of you that feels judged.

In truth, you are not "human" or "Divine." You are both. You are *all*. For *all* is all there is.

Complex? Yes. Confusing? Perhaps. But truth.

It is not necessary for you to "figure it out," or to dissect the ways of the Universe until you can understand the whys and the hows and the whats. All that is necessary is for you to feel the truth. We are all one. We are all Divine.

We sit here, watching you, as you evolve your senses and perceptions of what it means to be "human" and "Divine."

Science, religion, philosophy all try to make sense of it. And we say to you, "Breathe. Fill your heart. Listen. Be at peace." In the space you create, you will find the answers (and they won't be anything you can explain).

We breathe the Divine, and the Divine breathes us.

Look to your Divine heart…it's all in there.

~ The Angelic Realm

20

A MASTERFUL BAKER

The ego sees the world outside and says, "This is how things are." We ask you to look to the inside world to recognize "this is what can be."

A burning desire bursting from your heart is a sign that this creation is ready to enter the birthing process, ready to come into the world and be experienced in your reality, and for you to have exactly what you desire. That desire was placed there by God (Source – Divine) so that you may create and experience all the joys the world has to offer.

Like a cake baking in the oven, you can smell its delicious aroma and your mouth waters in anticipation of tasting and experiencing it.

Do you doubt that the cake is there when you smell its aroma and know the baking process has begun?

You crave it. You can taste it. You know that you had the idea to make the cake and you placed it in the oven with care, anticipating its completion.

It is the same with any creation you make, even those created from the unseen realms.

A creation begins to come into existence as soon as you experience the first moment of awareness of that true, burning desire from your heart. It is the exact moment the seeds become planted and the potential for its creation in the 3D world becomes possible.

Yet, how often do you doubt, give into fear, or tell yourself that you aren't deserving of this creation? It is this doubt, fear, and sense of unworthiness that can prevent your "cake of creation" from rising and being ready to enjoy.

Your sense of unworthiness, your fear, and your doubt can cause the cake to never finish baking, or even to burn and turn out very differently than you had planned.

You are a Divine creator, a masterful baker in the realm of creation.

Trust that your burning desire, from your heart, is a message from God, from Source Energy, that this is possible. That burning desire is encoded with information and all the ingredients you require to complete the baking.

Everything that is required to complete your recipe is contained within the encoding of this desire.

Follow the recipe…follow your desire.

As you hold this energy of desire and passion and joy and love for what you are creating from your heart, the baking happens, as if by magic. You will be guided along the way, given the steps and the guidance you need to complete.

You do not need to compare your recipe with other recipes. You do not need to use your ego-mind to think of how you could make it better. Everything is contained in the energy of your desire.

And we promise you, as you follow this recipe of Divine desire from your heart, you will create the best tasting cake you have ever made.

We can't wait to enjoy it with you. For we know what a masterful baker you are.

~ The Angelic Realm

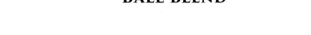

LIMITLESS DESIRES DIFFUSER / ROLLER BALL BLEND

1 drop Cardamom Essential Oil
1 drop Ginger Essential Oil
1 drop Vetiver Essential Oil
2 drops Geranium Essential Oil

This diffuser blend surrounds you in the warm, spicy, and floral aromas of creation and desire. It opens and massages the energy of the root, sacral, and heart chakras allowing the energy of your true desires to rise up into your energy field so they can be released into the world.

Use this blend when you need to reconnect with the energy of your passion and desires; when you have lost your way and are struggling to believe that your dreams and wishes could actually come true.

To make a 5mL roller ball blend to wear topically, add the drops of oil to a 5mL roller bottle, then top with fractionated coconut oil (or other carrier oil). Apply to your heart and lower abdomen, just above the pubic bone.

When diffusing or using this blend topically, take a moment to feel, sense, imagine, or think about the energy of passion and creation rising from your lower chakras (beneath your navel) to your heart, where it joins the energy of love and then bursts out into the world. This activates the energy of forward movement in your energy field required for the birthing of the energy that will one day be the fulfillment of your desires.

A look at the oils in this blend:

Cardamom – The Oil of Objectivity. This oil helps you to release any feelings of anger, frustration, or blame that may arise when your desires do not manifest as rapidly as you wish.

Ginger – The Oil of Empowerment. This oil empowers you to take complete responsibility for your life circumstances and to continue moving forward with passion and purpose.

Vetiver – The Oil of Centring and Descent. This oil helps to ground you in the present moment, and to connect with the energy of your thoughts and emotions. It assists in resolving any limiting beliefs or feelings that are getting in the way of the achievement of your desires.

Geranium – The Oil of Love and Trust. This oil provides emotional support and restores the flow of love where it has been disrupted. It restores feelings of trust that everything will turn out as it is meant to. "This or something better."

21

FILLING THE BANKS OF ENERGY

There is so much beauty around you. There is so much to be happy for and to live for.

You can look around the world and see the dark, the hatred, the greed, the envy, and the terrors all around. Or you can look to a higher level and see the beauty, the strength, the forgiveness, and the blessings that are being multiplied in every moment.

We ask you to see the beauty! See with the eyes of the innocent child, seeing magic and wonder everywhere.

Then ask yourself: *"How can I make this world even more beautiful? How can I add more love, more fun, more joy?"*

Be mindful not to take on the pain and burdens and suffering of others, for in that way you cannot help them. By taking on the energy of their pain, you are lowering your own vibration and this contributes to a continuing decline of the energy of love. A focus on lack and fear only brings more of the same.

Instead, look to yourself and say: *"How can I brighten the world, beginning with me? How can I bring more light here?"*

For as you do this, you create a ripple effect that spreads out beyond you. It touches those around you. It permeates into the very fabric of existence that ties us all together.

By spreading more energy of love, hope, joy, and light, into the world you are affecting change at a level that may not be immediately seen, but is deeply felt.

This higher vibrational energy enters into the "banks" of planetary energy, and the balance begins to shift.

So, we ask you to be mindful of the energy you wish to contribute to the world. And to know that it is safe and okay to be happy and healthy and well, even when others aren't.

For your task, Divine child, is to change the world by filling the banks of energy with the energy of love and joy and happiness.

Can you do this today? Are you ready to create a shift?

We are here with you, always.

~ The Angelic Realm

22

A BEAUTIFUL KALEIDOSCOPE

Do you know how beautiful you are? How loved you are? How infinitely supported you are?

If you were able to see yourself like we do, you would never doubt your worth. You would never doubt your place in the world. You would never doubt anything about yourself at all!

We see you as a kaleidoscope of energy, beautiful from every angle. As you go through your day, your week, your month…the energy patterns shift and change.

The emotions of fear, distrust, anger, pain, and sadness create one type of pattern. The emotions of joy, happiness, love, elation, forgiveness, and gratitude create another type of pattern.

All patterns are beautiful – all make up the magical tapestry that is your life and your human experience.

The important thing to remember is that the patterns in the kaleidoscope are constantly changing. As you turn the kaleidoscope, new patterns emerge. It is this movement and ever-changing patterns that make a kaleidoscope so beautiful and enticing to watch. Every image and pattern is part of the whole. Every turn contributes to the movement and creation of the next pattern.

We love you. All of you.

The challenging experiences and the great ones are all part of your wonderful and wild kaleidoscope. All are necessary, and all carry beauty in their own way.

The next time you notice yourself judging the pattern you are in, remember it is instrumental in moving you to the next pattern, and there is beauty in all of it.

You are dearly loved. Always.

~ The Angelic Realm

23

LAY DOWN YOUR BURDENS

Be at peace. Surrender. Release all the fears, burdens, and worries you are carrying and that weigh so heavily on your heart. Allow us to carry them for you, that you may be free to rest awhile.

Lay down your head and heart and allow yourself to feel the freedom and peace that is present without these fears and worries. Feel the expansion of your soul as you allow us to enter in and support you fully.

Give the intent for your worries and cares to be placed on "pause" for the next few moments, to allow you to breathe deeply into the feeling of what it is to be without them. Don't worry, they will still be there if you choose to keep them.

How does it feel?

We ask you now to make a choice. ***What worries are you ready to let go of, once and for all? What are you ready to give up?*** Let us continue to hold those for you, so you can find peace in your being.

For your work here is important, your presence on Earth matters.

Let us carry this for you. You have more important work to do.

In Love and Service,

~ The Angelic Realm

24

THE PARADOX OF CHOICE

Choice. The paradox of free will.

You have the power to make any choice you desire; yet sometimes you feel like it would be easier if things were just laid out for you, ensuring the right path was always the one chosen and followed.

We say to you – all choices lead to the same path, eventually. Some paths just take longer to travel than others. Don't fret so much when making a choice. Know that you will always get to where you want to go…eventually.

The easiest path, however, will come when you can silence the voices of fear, doubt, judgment (of others and of self), and all the worries you hold inside. Imagine them being released into the wind, tossing them up to be carried away, so only the clearest, easiest path in line with the resonance of your heart and soul will be shown.

This takes practice, for the voice of the ego-mind can be strong, but you can call on us for help to hold the energy of stillness and peace around you as you do your work. For we cannot do this work for you, but we can be a comforting presence as you make your choice.

As you choose to release and to see the clearest path, we surround you with our love, radiating this love into your heart and energetic field to ease the process of transforming the fears and doubts and worries.

Try it sometime. Know that you are not alone. Will that make the choice seem easier? Well, we say that is up to you!

~ The Angelic Realm

EYES OPEN DIFFUSER / ROLLER BALL BLEND

2 drops Lime Essential Oil
1 drop Lemongrass Essential Oil
1 drop Marjoram Essential Oil
1 drop Blue Tansy Essential Oil

This diffuser blend helps to cleanse away all mental energy that is blocking you from seeing your path forward. It removes the threads of residual darkness from old mental patterns and self-sabotage and turns your mind to more positive thoughts. Use this blend whenever you don't know which way to go, when your thoughts are muddled with confusion or too many choices. It will restore feelings of trust in yourself, in the Divine, and in the flow of life.

To make a 5mL roller ball blend to wear topically, add the drops of oil to a 5mL roller bottle, then top with fractionated coconut oil (or other carrier oil). Apply to the base of your skull, along the spine at the back of the neck, and on your temples.

When diffusing or using this blend topically, take a moment to feel, sense, imagine, or think about the energy of any old mental patterns that have been keeping you stuck and holding you hostage. Visualize them being carried away by the angels and replaced with a golden halo of light and discernment.

A look at the oils in this blend:

Lime – The Oil of Zest for Life. This oil helps you to release an over-analytical or over-intellectual view of life and restore balance with the energy of the heart. With the mind and heart working in unison, it is much easier to see the next steps on your path.

Lemongrass – The Oil of Cleansing. This oil helps you to release old, limiting beliefs and thought patterns from the past. It cleanses and activates the energy of the brow/third eye chakra, enabling you to "see" more clearly.

Marjoram – The Oil of Connection. This oil helps to restore feelings of trust and openness in relationships, including your relationship with yourself and your relationship with the Divine.

Blue Tansy – The Oil of Inspired Action. This oil helps to release resistance to change and transformation. It assists you in moving forward, overcoming patterns of resistance and retreat, so that you can reach for the highest expression of yourself.

25

THE ENEMY WITHIN

D o you feel lost or alone? Are you afraid?

Spreading your wings and soaring in this new energy can feel overwhelming, because it is a place you have never been before.

You have overcome hurdles in the past. Yes! And the energies of what are occurring and transforming on the planet now are of a much more refined level.

No longer are the challenges those of walking through the mud of the 3D world. Now the challenges and struggles are much more about what lies within yourself.

The enemy is not from without. There is not some foreign external element that must be fought or overcome.

In this time of heightened transformation and conscious evolution, the enemy exists purely within. The fear, the doubt, the lack of self-worth, the projections, the misunderstandings....

Do you see that everyone is reacting to his or her own perceptions from within? These perceptions then turn into actions in the outside world.

Do not be fooled by what you see – the world right now is just a reflection of the fear, the old cords and ties that hold people to the old ways and old belief systems. These are crumbling now and this causes much confusion.

If you perceive your life to be threatened, it will be. If you perceive peace and joy and abundance, you can have that, too.

It is time to rebuild from the heart and the conscious, spiritual mind.

For, you see, once you are attuned to the energy of potentials and possibilities around you, you are able to respond to each situation more fully and completely. You are able to align your internal world into one of peace, love, abundance, and joy.

Then you turn to the outside world and see if what is around you is a vibrational match for what you have created inside. If the answer is no, you simply walk away and find a place that is. Simple changes can be very powerful.

You cannot change anyone but you. And yet your inner beauty will shine through to the world and affect all those that you meet. Your inner light will begin to shine with the purity of all that you carry inside.

It starts with you.

~ The Angelic Realm

26

SPARKLES OF WONDER

There is so much for you to see and experience in this world. So much for you to drink in. Yet how much are you allowing this to happen? ***How much do you truly see when you look around at the world?***

You are so stuck in what you "should" be doing, that you fail to see the magic, the opportunities and the possibilities all around you. There are sparkles of wonder dancing right in front of your face, yet you cannot see them due to the veil of illusion that covers your eyes.

We say this with no judgment, only love. It's time to shake things up!

It's natural for you to see the world in this way. It's how things have evolved for eons of humanity. And now, you get to be the excited ones who evolve beyond the veil; you get to see what is on the other side.

As the veil thins, there is more for you to see. More for you to experience. There is more than ever before. All you have to do is open your eyes.

Take a moment now to open your heart. Breathe deeply and give the intent to perceive all the wonders around you. Be still with your heart and your connection with the Divine.

It will take time, but over the next few weeks, months and years, you will begin to build a new world for yourself. This new world begins with the conscious intent from within you to see this new world. Then to practice every day – catch yourself when you are caught up in the thoughts of "what if," "what should," "what would" and surrender instead to *seeing what is.*

Let the magic begin!

~ The Angelic Realm

27

THE PATH FORWARD

There is nothing you cannot do. Truly! If you have a clear, strong desire born of your heart, then it is possible.

There is nothing you cannot be. Truly! If you can imagine yourself in the position, then it is possible.

There is nothing you cannot have. Truly! If you can feel the energy of having these things in your grasp, then it is possible.

The most important element in the creation of your desires is to *keep moving forward*. Even when you do not see the path. Even when you are unsure of the way. Hold your energy and focus on the desires you have at hand, and walk forward in faith that all will be delivered and you will not be alone as you walk (for you are never alone).

The path you have seen for yourself may not be as you imagine it will be, but it is possible.

Trust, be open, then wait. The path will be shown to you as you take the first steps.

Each day you awaken, you have the ability to step forward again and again. Never stop. Keep your faith. Lean into the energy of love. Feel your desires. Keep moving.

The path is forward.

~ The Angelic Realm

28
FOLLOW YOUR DREAMS

There is nothing you could ever say or do that would change the love and compassion we have for you.

When you feel scared and alone, remember that. When you consider doing things that may seem out of the ordinary or different than the accepted norms, know we are standing here with you, too.

Breathe deeply and feel our presence.

Let the sounds and feelings of our unending love and support be heard and felt. Know that we walk with you on this path. We surround you. We encourage you. And we are here if you stumble and fall. We will walk beside you as you pick yourself back up and carry on.

For we know you will be successful. We know you must succeed. Because you are made of stars and love and magic.

The only way to fail is to fail to see how truly magnificent you are.

Are you ready to rock the world?

You do so by your very presence. Go out there and follow your dreams! We are watching and cheering you on!

~ The Angelic Realm

ANGEL'S GIFT DIFFUSER / ROLLER BALL BLEND

2 drops Lemon Essential Oil
1 drop Wild Orange Essential Oil
1 drop Douglas Fir Essential Oil
1 drop Helichrysum Essential Oil
1 drop Thyme Essential Oil

This diffuser blend washes away all of the feelings of fear, lack, and unworthiness that you carry inside, reminding you instead of your Divine angelic self. It helps you rise above the limitations you have placed upon yourself and cleanses away longstanding patterns and energies that are preventing you from fully taking charge of your life.

As you use this blend, you will be surrounded by the loving energy of the angels, singing your praises and reminding you that the trials and challenges of human life are only obstacles to be faced in order to help you remember the greatness of who you are.

To make a 5mL roller ball blend to wear topically, add the drops of oil to a 5mL roller bottle, then top with fractionated coconut oil (or other carrier oil). Apply to your heart, the back of your neck, and the soles of your feet.

When diffusing or using this blend topically, take a moment to feel, sense, imagine, or think about all the gifts and blessings that exist in your life. Remind yourself that even in challenging times, there is always a solution to every problem. Breathe in and feel the loving energy

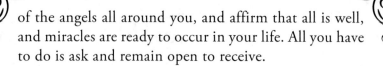

of the angels all around you, and affirm that all is well, and miracles are ready to occur in your life. All you have to do is ask and remain open to receive.

A look at the oils in this blend:

Lemon – The Oil of Focus. This oil is instantly cleansing and uplifting to the mind and emotions. It inspires feelings of joy, lightness, confidence, and energy.

Wild Orange – The Oil of Abundance. This oil inspires creativity and uplifts your mood. It helps to release the mindset of lack and scarcity and restores feelings of joy and flow in your life.

Douglas Fir – The Oil of Generational Wisdom. This oil helps you to break free from negative patterns passed down by generations. It inspires you to follow your own conscience and forge a new path.

Helichrysum – The Oil for Pain. This oil offers strength and wisdom as you heal through old wounds and pain. It reminds you of the strength you have built up by overcoming challenges. It carries the energy of rebirth and renewal.

Thyme – The Oil of Releasing and Forgiving. This oil cleanses the emotional body and encourages the energy of forgiveness, both of yourself and of those who have hurt you. Through this forgiveness, your soul is freed to continue its growth and evolution unhindered.

29

YOUR LIGHT

Just as the sun shines brightly in the sky, so do we see the essence and purity of your soul light.

Even when you are feeling at your most low, or feel that you have been "dimmed" in the world, we see the truth; we see the glorious light that resides within.

In order for you to have the impact in the world that you want to – whether to be a shining star of performing arts, a caring teacher, an inspiring speaker, a talented seamstress, or a wonderful mother, father, lover, and friend – you need to see the same light that we do.

This light shines in all you do. It cannot be turned off. It can only be dimmed by your own self-doubt and fear.

So, the next time you are with a friend or family member, ask yourself: *"How can I shine my light right now? How can I show up and be the brightest me in this relationship?"*

The next time you are volunteering or working in your chosen field, ask yourself: *"What is my soul light asking of me right now? How am I meant to show up and shine?"*

As you begin to ask yourself these questions, you will begin to break down the walls and the fears that prevent you from seeing what we see. You will naturally feel the outpouring of your light and it comes in simple ways.

As you allow yourself to see the beautiful light inside, so, too, will others.

And then, you will shine as bright as the brightest star. It will feel so natural to you. Because it is!

~ The Angelic Realm

30

SHADOWS AND LIGHT

This is a time for you to go within and to seek out that which you truly desire. At no time in human history has there been this moment as there is right now – the specific time and date, with the specific energy, with the specific people incarnated on the planet. The energy is prime for change.

If you desire more peace on Earth, place this desire in your heart. Hold it with the image of a golden infinity symbol in your heart, broadcasting a balanced energy of giving and receiving – love and peace and joy and abundance – available for all.

Let your intentions be known to the Universe. Let us hear your call and the prayers in your heart, for we cannot intervene without your asking. You do not have to go it alone.

We are here, waiting to infuse the world with more light and more love. We are here to support you and guide you. We are here to love with you and to place the energy of Divine love all around you. But you must open the gates for us to enter. You must ask so that we may play our role. We do this willingly and with love, for that is our Divine mission.

As you open the gates for more love and joy to enter, be mindful of all that you are ready to release. Let go of the pain, fear, judgment, and shame you hold within. Honour all that you have experienced. Honour the pain and suffering of others. And do not get bogged down or lost in it. See it. Acknowledge it. Honour it. And transform it.

This is a time to see the shadows with the light, and to know that as the shadows cross over the light of the world, so, too, will the light return. Reflect, contemplate, and prepare for the new wave of light energy that is coming.

Do not turn your back on the shadows, for it is the contrast that allows for the new light to emerge. It is in the darkness that you will find a new path to the light. For you must.

You are a being of light, even though you feel lost at times. It is your natural state to seek out and return to the light, despite those who have fallen and are lost on the path. Do not allow their loss to become yours.

Today, what do you desire? Imagine these desires in your heart, energetic intentions of pure light and love, thrown out to the Universe and then the energy becomes amplified and returned to your heart, this beautiful figure eight shaped pathway.

Infinity highway.

We are ready to receive your requests. Thank you for playing your role in the ever-evolving consciousness of humanity.

~ The Angelic Realm

31

BREATH OF LIFE

Wherever you are right now and whatever you are doing, stop. Take a breath. Feel us surrounding you. The more you open to receive the blessings that surround you – through the breath – the more you will be open to continuously receive this Divine breath in every inhale you take.

Practice inhaling the golden light of Christ Consciousness – the Divine breath of All That Is.

Inhale this beautiful golden light, tinged with the energy of white and pink light of Divine compassion. Feel this entering through the nose and travelling to your lungs, to exchange with your blood, and move to every cell in your body.

Breath is life. Breath is love. Breath is joy.

Stop. Breathe. Receive.

As you practice this for just a few moments each day, you are training yourself to continuously receive this flow of abundant blessings. After a while, you will not even realize you are doing it!

Every breath becomes sacred. Every moment becomes Divine, even without thinking about it.

Imagine your world where you are in constant flow with All That Is, simply by breathing the air that you need to survive.

Guess what…you're already there!

~ The Angelic Realm

32

EMBRACING CHANGE

This is a time of new beginnings. You are asked to look at your current path and see where you would like to make course adjustments.

Just because you have always done things a certain way does not mean this is the way that things should always be done. By the time the Earth makes another trip around the sun, your life will be so different!

Embrace change every day, moving yourself one step closer to the way you desire things to be.

Change is good. Change is what you make of it. In every change, find the opportunity. The opportunity for growth, for new beginnings, and for unexpected blessings. For there is always something new for you to discover.

How will you embrace the change that is coming?

Will you face it head on, the captain of your own vessel, or will you fight it all the way and miss the many wonders and blessings that would be available to you on the way?

The choice is yours.

- The Angelic Realm

TIDES OF CHANGE DIFFUSER / ROLLER BALL BLEND

1 drop Sandalwood Essential Oil
1 drop Copaiba Essential Oil
1 drop Ginger Essential Oil
1 drop Tea Tree (Melaleuca) Essential Oil

This diffuser blend helps you to let go of the past and eliminate any fears of moving forward. It inspires you to make the necessary changes in your life for your continued growth and evolution. It strengthens your ability to discern what is right for you and helps you to develop healthy energetic boundaries.

To make a 5mL roller ball blend to wear topically, add the drops of oil to a 5mL roller bottle, then top with fractionated coconut oil (or other carrier oil). Apply to your heart, across your upper back and shoulders, and at the base of your spine. This will activate your "wings" and help you create a strong foundation as you "fly" forward.

When diffusing or using this blend topically, take a moment to feel, sense, imagine, or think about the changes that are calling you forward. Give gratitude for all that you have experienced in the past, and honour your courage to continue moving forward toward all that life has in store for you.

A look at the oils in this blend:

Sandalwood – The Oil Sacred Devotion. This oil helps to quiet the mind and assists you in hearing the voice of the Divine. It aids in releasing ties and attachment to the material world and to feel connected to the energy of All That Is.

Copaiba – The Oil of Unveiling. This oil assists you in overcoming feelings of shame, guilt, blame, and self-loathing from your past experiences. It brings you back to the Divine, where healing and connection can reveal to you the truth about the brilliant being of light that you are.

Ginger – The Oil of Empowerment. This oil empowers you to take complete responsibility for your life circumstances and to continue moving forward with passion and purpose.

Tea Tree (Melaleuca) – The Oil of Energetic Boundaries. This oil releases negative and toxic energetic baggage of all forms from your energy field. It assists in clearing away the old and creating new, healthier boundaries to support you as you move forward in life.

33

EMBRACING THE GRANDNESS OF IT ALL

How could you ever doubt your magnificence? We look at you and we ask this question.

We see your brilliance. We see the magic you carry in every fibre of your being. We know that you are a part of the Great Whole. We know who you are.

Yet you have forgotten.

At times you remember, we know. Times when you feel the grandness of it all. You see the stars, the sunset or sunrise, the beauty in the nature all around you, the laughter of a child.

And yet you see that as outside of yourself. You see all of that as wonders that exist but are fleeting.

We tell you that this is the grandness of what exists within you and around you all the time! It never ceases. Only your ability to tap into the truth of it wavers.

Today, let all of your senses come alive as you see, feel, taste, touch, smell, and *know* that you are Divine. You are part of the whole. You *are* whole.

Then notice how life begins to change all around you.

~ The Angelic Realm

34

DARING TO LIVE THE DREAM

Have you ever dreamed a dreamed so vividly that you woke up and realized that it must someday come true? The dream where everything turns out more wonderful than you could have imagined before?

Of course you have...for we have watched these dreams form and play out in your subconscious mind as you slept. We helped move the energy along.

You have experienced these dreams, from time to time, even if you don't have a recollection of them in the waking world.

We place these little visions of the future into your cellular memory so you will continue to be pulled forward, as if by some unseen force, toward the fulfillment and achievement of these dreams.

What stops them from coming true? Only you. Your doubts, fears, and uncertainties get in the way, like a magnet attracting all the worries and possibilities, which would make these dreams go unfulfilled.

The next time you catch yourself coming up with reasons you can't be, have, or do what you saw in your dream state, remember those dreams truly are a vision of reality, a track you are already on course for. And don't let yourself change course by creating the things that will get in the way.

Surrender and watch your life unfold exactly as you dreamed it would be!

~ The Angelic Realm

35

MOVING THROUGH THE VEIL OF ILLUSION

Nothing is as it seems. Things appear on the surface to be one way, but continuously prove to be otherwise as you step through the veil of illusion and see beyond duality into the light of truth. As you move through this period, things will seem as if they are upside down, topsy turvy, and almost as though there is a cosmic joke happening at your expense.

This is a realignment phase where everything is being cast aside that is not serving, but first must be made visible to your conscious mind for you to realize it is time to say goodbye.

As you enter this new phase of enlightened living, things will feel upset at times – ungrounded, in constant motion, and perhaps, vacant.

The feeling of not knowing what is coming next is a sign you are entering the void of creation, the holding place between the old world and the new.

Be at peace and know we are always with you, watching, guiding, supporting you in immeasurable ways.

Give in to the temptation to rest, to be free, and to do the things that seem impossible but also magical if they turn out. Experiment, have fun, and know you do not need to be attached to any outcome.

All is changeable right now. You are just finding your way, as a young child does when learning to walk. Things appear different. New muscles are required. New adjustments to be made.

There is no right or wrong when you start. There is only awareness of the circumstances and course correction toward more of what you like and away from what you don't like.

The rules are changing and it's time to rewrite your story. All is up for rewriting. Everything is possible. Nothing is static.

Now, more than ever, it is important to keep your energy clear. Cleanse your body, clear your energy, purify your mind. As you move forward, there will be more and more resistance to your freedom.

As you purify your vibration through thoughts and actions of love, you will be met with the old energies, which boast duality, conflict, and victimhood. Know that this is not you, but it is merely a reminder of what you are moving away from. We urge you not to attach meaning to these thoughts or circumstances, but only to notice them and say, "no thank you."

Call on us to cleanse your energy, to release attachments, to support your growth and evolution. All you have to do is give intent and we will be there.

In peace, love, and the expansion of your soul,

- The Angelic Realm

36

DO NOT BE AFRAID

D o not be afraid to show up in the world exactly as you are. You are safe, you are rooted, you are strong, and you are beautiful.

When you hide your light, you diminish your growth. When you hide your light, you rob the world of the magic of who you are and what you bring.

Don't hide. Show up. Be seen. Be strong. Be brave. *Be Free.*

~ The Angelic Realm

FREE TO BE ME DIFFUSER / ROLLER BALL BLEND

1 drop Ylang Ylang Essential Oil
1 drop Oregano Essential Oil
1 drop Patchouli Essential Oil
1 drop Wintergreen Essential Oil

This diffuser blend is a powerful recipe for transformation and growth. It cleanses away the "sticky" energy of attachment to people, situations, and patterns, which are not in full alignment with your purpose. It reminds you of the power you wield as an incarnated being and assists you in transcending the lower vibrations of fear and ego, returning you to a state of innocence, joy, and wonder. From this place, you are free to be exactly who you are.

To make a 5mL roller ball blend to wear topically, add the drops of oil to a 5mL roller bottle, then top with fractionated coconut oil (or other carrier oil). Apply to your feet, across the chest, and along the spine at the back of the neck. If you have sensitive skin, you may wish to dilute this blend by adding the same number of drops to a 10mL roller bottle. (Note: Avoid this blend if you are on blood thinners or have a sensitivity to methyl salicylates.)

When diffusing or using this blend topically, take a moment to feel, sense, imagine, or think about your energy rising up from beneath your feet, up your legs, along your torso, out your hands, and the top of your head. Give the intent to activate the fullness of *who you*

are and to live from this place unapologetically. Experience the freedom that this affords you and enjoy!

A look at the oils in this blend:

Ylang Ylang – The Oil of the Inner Child. This oil acts mainly on the heart energy, releasing negative feelings and heavy-heartedness. It restores you to a feeling of childlike innocence and openness.

Oregano – The Oil of Humility and Non-Attachment. This is a powerful oil that cuts away any energetic attachments and transforms rigidity you may be holding onto. It quickly and forcefully expels any energy that is not in alignment with the essence of your being.

Patchouli – The Oil of Physicality. This oil helps you to become fully present in your body, encouraging feelings of confidence and groundedness. It helps you to feel at peace and at home in your physical body.

Wintergreen – The Oil of Surrender. This oil helps you to let go of the need to know everything and to surrender to the energy of your higher self and the Divine. It reminds you that you are never alone and you are loved and protected, always.

37
GIVE THANKS

Gratitude. The most powerful emotion. With two small words – thank you – you can move mountains.

Today, we invite you to give thanks for all that you have, all that you are, and all that you ever will be. Through this energy of gratitude (and the energy of love that is forever tied with it), you will be creating new pathways and threads in your life story.

Every time you give thanks, you strengthen the threads of life that carry you toward more of the same. It is the recurring thanks that strengthen these pathways into certainties.

Whenever you feel your faith wavering and doubt setting in, give thanks for that which you desire, as if it were already made manifest. The energy that outpours from your heart and soul in the act of giving thanks will reawaken your faith and courage to take the steps that are required to achieve the fulfillment of the task you have been given.

We thank you for your courage, your devotion, and your love. We give thanks for you and your place in the world. We give thanks for our connection with you. For we could not truly fulfill our part without our connection with you, just as our role in your path is required for the fullest expression of your gifts and talents and path in this life.

We are all one. Give thanks.

~ The Angelic Realm

38

REMEMBER YOUR POWER

P ower. Whenever you feel afraid, sad, or lonely take a moment to remember the deep power you hold within.

Connect with your breath and feel into your core energy, the central column of light and energy that runs through your entire being. Feel into the truth of who you are.

There is nothing you cannot do, be, or have. The key is to be honest with yourself about why you want it, and what your heart is calling for you to do to achieve and receive it.

For your heart knows the way. And when you align your pure Divine heart with your Divine focus and Divine action, everything is possible.

Breathe in.

Feel the strength and power of you.

Surrender to the will of the Divine.

Let yourself be shown the way.

As you do this, all your desires will be made manifest through focused and specific action inspired by the energy of your Divine heart, your true self.

~ The Angelic Realm

39

THE RECALIBRATION OF YOUR ENERGY FIELD

The changes you are experiencing in your body now are a reflection of your willingness to let go and to surrender to the Divine plan. As the energy rises on the planet toward a greater consciousness, there is a lot to be accomplished. New energy patterns are being downloaded to you and all of humanity now, and there are those who may choose not to receive them.

This is a gift – a gift of higher consciousness, higher knowing, and a map to more compassion, truth, and love for all.

And, as always, the choice is yours.

As you experience these changes and the recalibration within your energy field, you will also experience some aches and pains in your physical body along the way.

Some of these are merely part of the realignment process, and you may ask us to support you or to "turn down the volume" whenever you choose. This will not affect the final outcome. It will merely allow for a unique adjustment to your specific frequency and energetic needs. Do not be afraid to ask. We are here to support and serve you on your journey to more love.

Where you feel the most resistance, you will experience the most symptoms. If you are feeling bloated, achy, tired, or disoriented during this process, know that this is simply a measure of your unwillingness to surrender control and be in the flow with the Divine and your soul.

As you breathe into your body, raise your hands in prayer, and close your eyes in meditation you will find the peace and stillness that will bring you back to the truth of who you are and help you shift more gracefully to hold more of this wholeness in your body.

Fear not. We are here with you always, guiding the way. All you have to do is be open to the possibilities and ask for clarification and support when you need it. We will not leave you unattended.

We are here. Loving you. Always.

~ The Angelic Realm

40

A NEW PORTAL OPENS

Rest, dear one. Allow yourself to rest and take in all the changes you are now experiencing. A big portal has just opened and new waves of energy are coming down onto the planet now. This may leave you feeling more tired than usual, disoriented, and even experiencing waves of nausea as the energy expands and integrates within your being. All is well as you learn to understand the new waves of light and energy, which are merging with your physicality now.

Be open to new insights and awareness as you welcome in these new energies. Rest and allow the integration to occur. You may feel waves of energy and motivation followed by waves of fatigue and a requirement for deep rest. Trust your body and ride the waves. This is a time of joy and celebration! It is also a time of rest and incorporating these new aspects of your being into your conscious and physical reality.

As always, we are here guiding and supporting you. Call on us to assist with this integration period. Know that you are dearly loved and cared for. This is a time of great renewal! Be at peace.

~ The Angelic Realm

REST AND RECALIBRATION DIFFUSER / ROLLER BALL BLEND

2 drops Frankincense Essential Oil
1 drop Lemongrass Essential Oil
1 drop Melissa Essential Oil

This diffuser blend offers a quiet space for you to rest when the energy of the world becomes too much. It supports the energy of integration and renewal, allowing your cells and energy field the space that is required for higher evolutionary changes to occur. It allows for a "pause" in the swirling energy all around you so that in the stillness, you can find your balance again.

To make a 5mL roller ball blend to wear topically, add the drops of oil to a 5mL roller bottle, then top with fractionated coconut oil (or other carrier oil). Apply to your brow (forehead), across your chest, and down the spine.

When diffusing or using this blend topically, take a moment to feel, sense, imagine, or think about the energy of peace and stillness. Notice the feeling of total relaxation and stillness, which envelops you as you give the intent to take a pause from the world to allow your body, mind, and spirit to heal.

A look at the oils in this blend:

Frankincense – The Oil of Truth. This oil helps to dissolve the lies and illusions that keep you trapped and hold you back from living life to the fullest. It connects you back to your Divine light.

Lemongrass – The Oil of Cleansing. This oil helps you enter a state of energetic cleansing and healing. From this place, you can more readily release old, stagnant patterns and energy and make room for new higher vibrational alignment to enter.

Melissa – The Oil of Light. This oil awakens you to your Divine light and assists you in letting go of all darkness and shadow, which are preventing you from living in the full essence of who you are.

41

THE DOOR AHEAD OF YOU

Ask and you shall receive. Knock and the door shall be opened. These truths are still in effect and are yours to consider.

When you take guided action from your heart, launching your desires out in front of you, you are in the act of asking. It is the energy of desire, paired with motion toward your goal, which creates the certainty that what you are asking for will be accomplished.

Simply asking without movement will not yield results. Similarly, movement without a goal will not yield results.

Clarity and focus are requirements, as well as a full heart and a willingness to follow the threads of passion that pull you forwards in alignment with your Divine will.

Then, as you move further along the path toward your goal, continuing to ask, to take action, and move forward, when the time comes and the door is in front of you, you need only to be brave enough to knock on it, to know you are worthy, and to walk through it and into the full manifestation of what you desire. And from this place, you begin again. On to the next desire, the next journey, the next door.

But always ask. Move forward. Follow the passion and pull of your heart. Don't be afraid to knock once you get before that door. The very fact that you made it far enough to see the door ahead of you means you are worthy and deserving of what is behind it.

As you open the door and take in all that you see, you are perfectly positioned to move forward on to the next refinement of your will – to the next step in your evolution.

The only requirement is that you start.

Today, what are you asking for? What are you moving toward? Where does your heart pull you?

Take a moment to breathe into your heart, listen to the silence, and allow the answers to well up within you.

As always, we are here guiding and supporting you. Showering you with love and cheering you along your path.

~ The Angelic Realm

42

ON FEELING ANXIOUS, AFRAID, AND UNCERTAIN

Whenever you feel overwhelmed with fear, anxiety, or uncertainty, take a deep breath and allow these feelings to wash over you, just for a moment.

Allow yourself to feel deeply into the fear and become awash with all that is coming up against you. See that you are still standing once that minute has passed – the fear has not been able to knock you over or conquer you.

You are still here. You are still strong.

From this point of allowing the fear and anxiety to have its moment, you have stopped fighting against it, and instead acknowledged and accepted this part of your being.

You have said, "I see you. I love you. I accept you." You have allowed the voice of fear to be heard, so now it may fall silent again.

When you fight against the fear, and try to drive it down, it just becomes louder. All it asks for is an acknowledgement, to say, "Yes, I see you. I am here with you. We are okay."

Just like a small child, the voice of fear wants to be seen, acknowledged, and comforted.

From this place of acknowledgment, together, you can see the calmer waters and the new beach that has been created by allowing that wave of fear to pass over and through you. You have allowed the fear to swell and crash and become gentle and soft again.

It is in this way that you can move forward – little by little – stronger and stronger each day, not in spite of your fears, but because of them.

~ The Angelic Realm

43

CELEBRATE!

Celebrate! Celebrate all that is, all that you are, all that you have done, and all that is yet to come!

In this celebration, you will find peace, joy, worthiness, and resilience to keep moving forward. As you celebrate your successes, your triumphs, and especially your willingness to get up again after a fall, you will bring more energy of abundance and glory to you.

For you truly are the creator of your reality. Even as you falter and fall, you are sending signals out to the Universe, and we angels must heed your call.

We never send you what you do not want, but we can stop sending you what you say you desire if your desire becomes clouded by fear, anger, hatred, self-doubt, or self-loathing.

Don't want success? Love? Joy? Peace? Feel you don't deserve it? Feel it's not possible? That you can't achieve it, receive it, or believe it? We know you can. You can have it. You deserve it. And in fact, it is already yours! But we must heed your wishes for we are faithful servants of the Divine energy of love. The energy that says we must honour and respect your wishes and help you create the world you desire.

So celebrate, don't negate! For then we can celebrate with you and *bring you more!*

Always more. More love. More joy. More abundance. More health. More peace. More passion. More certainty.

It's all there. Start where you are. Then *celebrate every little thing*. It will all add up and soon you will see that you are in a constant state of celebration…***imagine what your life can look like then.***

~ The Angelic Realm

44
BREATHE

B reathe. Just breathe.

This is your task for today.

Feel the air of Spirit enter your lungs and flow through you as you allow yourself to be filled with this Holy breath.

Inhale love. Exhale peace, compassion, right-mindedness.
Inhale love. Exhale pain, suffering, sorrow.
Inhale love. Exhale unjustness, confusion, and apathy.
Inhale love. Exhale loss.
Inhale love. Exhale regret.
Inhale love. Exhale anger.
Inhale love. Exhale relief, peace, remembering.
Inhale love. Exhale love.
Inhale love. Exhale love.
Inhale love. Exhale love.

And so it is.

~ The Angelic Realm

BREATH OF SPIRIT DIFFUSER / ROLLER BALL BLEND

1 drop Eucalyptus Essential Oil
1 drop Thyme Essential Oil
2 drops Siberian Fir Essential Oil

This diffuser blend provides a deep experience of Divine breath and inspiration. It physically clears the pathways for more oxygen to enter the lungs, and with it, brings the energy of Spirit. This blend is particularly useful when you need to "breathe new life" into your spiritual practice or when you feel you are disconnected from the life-giving energy of Divine source. It allows you to remember that through breath, we are all unified and connected to the energy of the One.

To make a 5mL roller ball blend to wear topically, add the drops of oil to a 5mL roller bottle, then top with fractionated coconut oil (or other carrier oil). Apply across your chest to open the airways. Breathe deeply.

When diffusing or using this blend topically, take a moment to feel, sense, imagine, or think about breathing in the energy of the Divine. Experience the connection between the Divine without, carried upon the molecules of air, and the Divine within, housed within every cell of your being. Allow these two expressions of the Divine to mingle and fill you with the experience of being at one with your Divine source.

A look at the oils in this blend:

Eucalyptus – The Oil of Wellness. This oil helps you to dispel any beliefs or attachments to illness. It reminds you that you have the ability to heal yourself and reconnects you to the power of Divine health, which you carry within every cell of your body.

Thyme – The Oil of Releasing and Forgiving. This oil provides deep cleansing of stagnant energies that may prevent you from taking in all that life has to offer. It helps you to release and forgive all those who have hurt you, creating space for new experiences based on love, tolerance, and peace.

Siberian Fir – The Oil of Aging and Perspective. This oil helps to transform feelings of loss, grief, and regret. It offers support during times of transition and allows you to breathe deeply knowing that you are loved, supported, and watched over at all times.

45

TRUE LOVE

You have everything you need to make this next period either the most successful, or the most challenging.

You.

You decide.

Where will you spend your time focusing? On the potentials of success and growth and learning, or on the potentials of all that can go wrong?

At every moment, your energy is ripe for recalibration and a return to love, yet we see many who choose to dwell on the stress, fear, and pain.

We say to you today – you have a choice!

See not just the pain, but see the opportunity to grow, to love, to nurture, and to restore the energy of love, faith, and peace in all that you do.

For the choice is yours. See love or see pain. It's that simple. And yes, you can see love even as you delve into the feeling and depths of pain. In fact, that is the most profound love of all.

Do not hide from love in your fear.

Do not hide from your fear in a sense of overzealous and fabricated love.

Bring them both together. Love through your fears and pain. Acknowledge and accept that they are part of the story…then choose to live and see the face of love anyway.

You, beloved being, are all of it. But above it all, you are *love*.

~ The Angelic Realm

46
THE ENERGY OF FORGIVENESS

The energy of forgiveness is a natural state of being for an open heart, and yet you forget and make it so much more difficult than it needs to be.

You hold on to the idea that forgiveness releases another from their burdens and leaves you in pain; that in forgiving another you are letting them "off the hook" for their actions, or that you are saying what they did was acceptable. These are not truths.

Forgiveness is a way of becoming right with yourself again. To no longer allow the energy of anger, fear, and pain in your heart. Forgiveness releases you from your burdens. It has little effect energetically on the other person unless they allow it to.

For energy is a two-way street. You can forgive another, but have they forgiven themselves? Are they able to accept the forgiveness, see the lessons, and move into a higher state of being, resolving the energetic disturbances of the moment?

That, dear one, is their task, and is independent of your forgiveness.

And the same goes for you...*are you able to forgive yourself? For your actions, for your inaction, for making the wrong choice, for trusting the wrong person, for forgetting to put yourself first?*

Freedom is there. Love is present. The energy of All That Is exists in this sacred moment of forgiveness.

What do you choose today? Are you ready to forgive?

Take a moment to tune into the energy of forgiveness in your heart and let it pour out, like a beautiful emerald green ray of light into the Universe. Forgive as much as you can. Forgive everyone you can. Release yourself from your burdens.

Then turn that beautiful emerald green ray of light and forgiveness back into yourself. Allow it to penetrate into your sacred heart. Allow yourself to receive self-forgiveness.

Feel it, sense it, imagine it, and think it.

Then take a deep breath, give thanks, and go on with your day, remembering this powerful exercise can be repeated whenever you have need for more freedom and flow in your life.

And when those distractions come in, trying to tear you away from this great energy and flow you have created... forgive them, too.

~ The Angelic Realm

47
TRUST

Now is a time of patience. A time to sit in the stillness of all your creations and know that soon the harvest will be reaped.

You have sown the seeds so long ago, and now the time of waiting is upon you. Do not be disillusioned by the seeming absence of the fruits of your labours, for all is coming in due time.

Trust in the power of your plantings. Trust in the existence of the things you have called forth to you. Don't quit before the miracle occurs.

This is a time to remember to stay in vibrational alignment with all you are creating and to trust the time is coming when you will see the trees you have planted bear fruit.

Trust in yourself. Trust in Divine timing. Trust that you are loved and taken care of. Always.

~ The Angelic Realm

48

A TIME OF LIGHT AND POTENTIAL

As we enter this new time of light and potential, we remind you that you create your own reality. All that you desire is within your reach. All that you see around you is malleable by your thoughts, words, emotions, and actions.

For today, we invite you to feel the beauty that is all around you. Find it. Shine in the knowing that you are Divinely blessed in all ways. Focus on the love and the blessings all around you…see them, feel them, know they are real.

Allow the pain and the fears and the limitations from the past to fall away, even if just for a moment. As you focus on the love, you raise your vibration. From this state of pure love, you open the gateways of Divine creation within you.

Pour this love out into the world and release your desires as doves flying off in the wind. Trust that your messages will be received and be open to the signs and the messages that will be returning.

Your greatest gift lies in your ability to know and receive these messages. Whenever you feel out of alignment and unable to hear, sit in stillness and feel the love. Return to love, always.

For it is in this place that the mysteries of the Universe will open to you.

We are with you always, whispering in your ear. Get still. Feel the love. And you will hear us.

With unending love,

~ The Angelic Realm

DIVINE LIGHT DIFFUSER / ROLLER BALL BLEND

2 drops Lemon Essential Oil
1 drop Bergamot Essential Oil
1 drop Lavender Essential Oil
1 drop Sandalwood Essential Oil

This diffuser blend connects you to the energy of your Divine light. It awakens the energetic potential that exists within every cell of your Being and allows this light to be transmitted from your core and out into the world, lifting up and touching the lives of all those you come into contact with. Use this blend to enhance your power to heal and lift up the world. It is powerful when used alongside prayer and affirmations focused on world peace.

To make a 5mL roller ball blend to wear topically, add the drops of oil to a 5mL roller bottle, then top with fractionated coconut oil (or other carrier oil). Apply it to your heart, wrists, along your spine at the back of your neck, and the soles of your feet.

When diffusing or using this blend topically, take a moment to feel, sense, imagine, or think about your entire body and energy field being bathed in the light of the Divine. See this light permeating each and every cell and spreading out into the world, lighting up each individual on this planet, one at a time. Take a moment to congratulate yourself on your willingness to be an ambassador of light and love for the Divine.

A look at the oils in this blend:

Lemon – The Oil of Focus. This oil activates the energy of the solar plexus chakra to strengthen feelings of confidence and self-worth. It cleanses the entire mental body and restores feelings of personal power and certainty.

Bergamot – The Oil of Self-Acceptance. This oil releases stagnant energy and limiting beliefs and promotes feelings of self-love and self-acceptance. It is a beautiful oil to help remind you of the powerful, unlimited being that you are.

Lavender – The Oil of Communication and Calm. This oil dispels any feelings of fear, doubt, or unworthiness that blocks you from speaking out in the world. It inspires courage and confidence as you express yourself honestly through your voice.

Sandalwood – The Oil of Sacred Devotion. This oil helps to quiet the mind and assists you in hearing the voice of the Divine. It aids in releasing ties and attachment to the material world and to feel connected to the energy of All That Is.

49

DO NOT BE ROCKED
BY YOUR FEARS

Do not be rocked by your fears. Notice them, then breathe deeply into the stillness. See the truth that lies within.

These fears are merely your own mind attempting to block you from your greatness. Breathe into them and allow yourself to feel the energy of strength and resolve rise up within you, challenging these fears, as if to say, "no more!"

Let your strength and will be stronger than the voice of fear. You are stronger than you can imagine. Fear has no chance against the energy of love that you carry within.

Where will you choose love instead of fear today?

Breathe deeply as you ponder this. Then commit to yourself to see only love in the place of your fears.

We are with you always, walking hand in hand with the energy of your Divine self. You are never alone.

~ The Angelic Realm

50
JUST AS YOU ARE

You are surrounded by the most beautiful beings imaginable. They have chosen to be here, now with you. And yet still you doubt your worth.

Feel into the truth of who you are. Know that we are here to love, guide, and support you, yet we cannot do it alone. You are the key ingredient in this relationship. You are the one who has to say *yes* to allowing our assistance.

Today, we ask you to contemplate: *Are you ready to accept your worth? Are you ready to acknowledge that even though, at times, you may judge yourself harshly and tell yourself you are unworthy, you are worthy and deserving of so much more, just because you exist?*

When you are ready to say yes to this, you will be ready to feel more of us around you. Because it is not us who have pulled away and turned our backs on you. It is you who has turned your back on yourself.

We are here. Waiting. Always. To love, to guide, to support, and to rejoice in your being!

Just as you are.

~ The Angelic Realm

51

ALL IS WELL

When you feel fear for what is happening in your body, for your health, and for the challenges that may be starting or worsening, we say to you – be not afraid. Trust instead the process that is unfolding within you.

Focus on the message your body is sending you. Focus on listening intently to see what might be amiss. Focus on the awareness you now have.

Then focus on the love. On the light. On the certainty that you were made in your Creator's image – pure energetic perfection. That all is well and as it should be. This is an opportunity for you to sink into the truth of your existence and to reach for the highest levels of your mind (where thought creates reality) to find a solution to what you fear might be happening with you.

Seek out the support and the care you need, but always remember the acts of prayer, of affirmation, and of sending love to your cells are powerful beyond imagining.

Do not get stuck in the fear of a diagnosis, but instead use it as a jumping off point to find out more about yourself and where you need to lean in to more care, more awareness, and more love of self.

We are here with you, always. Watching. Waiting. Supporting. Guiding.

Call on us when you feel afraid and allow us to remind you that you are dearly loved and that you *are* love.

We will help you come home to yourself and know that all is well. Truly. All is well.

~ The Angelic Realm

52

THE KEYS TO YOUR DREAMS

As you flow through your days following the inner guidance that comes to you, you will find more peace, more ease, and more *fun* in your daily life. You often push against what the voice of your higher knowing tells you, pushing it aside as though it were a dream of something "too hard," "not for me," or "I could never do that."

But we say to you – if you are not able to do it, why would these thoughts and feelings pop up so often inside of you?

Any idea, dream, or passion you hold – even for the briefest moment that touches your heart – is for you.

It is merely your projection of your inadequacy – the false belief you have in your shortcomings – that pushes this aside and tells you that it isn't so.

What if, for one day, you followed all the guidance you received from us and your higher self? What if you leaned into the truth that we are showing you now...the truth of your power and potential that you have thus far been afraid to grasp?

Would you do this? Would you open your eyes and the doors to the future you have always dreamed of?

The keys have always been there, and we whisper to you constantly. It's time to stop brushing us aside and to say *yes* to the calling that you are receiving.

We await you in the glory of all that you are creating, and all that is possible for you *right now*.

With unending love,

~ The Angelic Realm

ENERGETIC CLEANSING DIFFUSER / ROLLER BALL BLEND

2 drops Lemon Essential Oil
1 drop Tea Tree (Melaleuca) Essential Oil
1 drop Cinnamon Bark Essential Oil
1 drop Spearmint Essential Oil

This diffuser blend is wonderful to use when you want to "disconnect" from lower energies, people, situations, or negative and repeating thought patterns. It cleanses your energy field, purifies your thoughts, and uplifts your moods, leaving you feeling clear and refreshed. Use this blend when you are feeling run down or fatigued with no explanation as it can lift unwanted energy that may be weighing you down.

To make a 5mL roller ball blend to wear topically, add the drops of oil to a 5mL roller bottle, then top with fractionated coconut oil (or other carrier oil). Apply it to your heart, your spine at the back of your neck, and to the soles of your feet.

When diffusing or using this blend topically, take a moment to feel, sense, imagine, or think about your entire body and energy field being cleansed and scrubbed clean of all that doesn't belong. Invite the angels in to bring you healing and uplifting energy and restore feelings of peace and well-being.

A look at the oils in this blend:

Lemon – The Oil of Focus. This oil helps to cleanse the mind of confusion and uncertainty. It activates the energy of the solar plexus chakra to strengthen feelings of confidence and self-worth. It cleanses the entire mental body and restores feelings of personal power and certainty.

Tea Tree (Melaleuca) – The Oil of Energetic Boundaries. This oil clears negative energy from toxic relationships, situations, and experiences. It purifies the energy body and removes any energetic residue from parasitic relationships, including the relationship with oneself. It restores and strengthens energetic boundaries.

Cinnamon – The Oil of Sexual Harmony. This oil helps to dispel fear of rejection, which can compromise the development of healthy boundaries in relationships. It empowers the energy of the sacral chakra and activates the flow of the creative potential, thus returning an individual to a state of oneness with the self.

Spearmint – The Oil of Confident Speech. This oil promotes emotional clarity in communication. It acts on the throat and third eye chakras to open spiritual communication and allow the return of clear vision and purpose, which may have been lost or muddied. It raises the energy out of lower vibrations and back to a state of high vibration and clarity.

REFERENCES AND RECOMMENDED RESOURCES

CITATIONS

(2017) Emotions & Essential Oils: A Reference Guide for Emotional Healing (Sixth Edition). Salt Lake City, UT: Enlighten Alternative Healing, LLC.

ESSENTIAL OILS

Join my Essential Alchemy Global doTERRA Tribe to gain access to the best oils on the planet plus receive additional education, resources, and support from me, including eBooks, video trainings, and a VIP Facebook Community. Visit www.mydoterra.com/rebeccaloach to get started.

ANGELIC ALCHEMY ESSENCE CARDS

This Divinely Inspired 33 Card Deck is infused with angelic blessings and healing activations to help you enhance your intuition, connect with the angels, align with your soul purpose, and uncover more of who you are. Available at www.rebeccaloach.com.

Angelic Wisdom, Inspiration, and Other Free Content

Join my mailing list to receive free weekly channeled Messages from the Angels delivered to you via email every Monday: www.rebeccaloach.com.

Join my private Facebook Community – Angelic Alchemy with Rebecca Loach – for inspiration, channeled messages, live videos, special offers, and other free content.

Alchemize Your Soul – Soulpreneur's Activation Program

Alchemize Your Soul is an experiential journey that will guide you to open up to your own intuitive gifts. Over four weeks, you'll receive powerful activations, healing energy, and opportunities to connect more deeply to the aspects of your self, soul, angels, guides, and higher consciousness.

If you are ready to say YES to yourself and your dreams, to open up to the fullest expression of who you are, and to invite more miracles and abundance into your life on a daily basis, this program is for you. Learn more at www.rebeccaloach.com

Lightning Source UK Ltd.
Milton Keynes UK
173379UK00001B/4/P